F

THE LITT

TRUE
STORIES
2

FHM PRESENTS...

THE LITTLE BOOK OF
TRUE STORIES
2

CARLTON
BOOKS

Thanks to FHM's readers for all their true stories

www.fhm.com

Desperate measures

Stewardess gets nasty shock

I was recently in Kefalonia, where the drainage system is so poor that a single flush of the toilet is woefully inadequate. On the last day we went out to the airport, where I was suddenly hit by serious stomach cramps. I found a secluded toilet just in time, releasing a ferocious explosion that reverberated around the room.

The stench was eye-watering, and to make matters worse, the flush was broken. As I strolled out, however, I walked straight into two air stewardesses doing their make-up in the mirror. I was in their rest room, but after their initial shock they saw the funny side, and promised not to tell. Then without warning, one of them walked into the cubicle. There was the briefest of pauses followed by an ear-deafening screech, at which point I sheepishly bolted for the plane, not even slowing down for customs.

Mobile Mistake

Texting lothario makes do

Not long ago, I met a girl in an internet chat-room. We got on well, so she gave me her mobile number and asked me to call. We exchanged a few texts, then a few days later she sent me a really filthy suggestion.I tapped in a suitable reply, searched through my address book for her name, and sent it. Her reply seemed a little strange but I didn't think anything more of it, as we were soon exchanging even more explicit texts. Eventually we decided to meet at a hotel, but when I got there at the appointed time who was there but my cousin. I said 'hi' and was about to ask what she was doing at the hotel, when it hit me; my cousin and the girl I'd originally been chatting to have the same first name, and both their numbers were stored in my phone. I didn't really know what to do, but my cousin's pretty attractive … so I went through with it with her instead.

Door slammer

Toilet becomes peep booth

Four years ago while attending college in Northern Ireland, myself and my girlfriend decided that we would take a week off college to visit both of our parents. As we settled into our train seats, it suddenly dawned on me that we would have to wait seven long days before having sex again, so I suggested that we nip off to the train toilet for a quick shag. I thought my woman would say no, but amazingly she agreed, and it wasn't long before we were both half-naked and I was slamming her doggy-style over the little sink. Just as I let rip up her back, I heard a cough behind me, and we turned to discover that, in our haste, we hadn't shut the door properly, giving the entire carriage a free porn show. To make things worse, the train was packed, and we had to stand for two and a half hours with everyone grinning and winking at us.

Private education

Darkness confuses student

In 1997, when I was still in the upper-sixth at school, several French student teachers arrived for teacher training. One night they all turned up in our local pub, and I ended up pulling one of the better-looking ladies of the group. After that, our relationship continued during school hours, every day at 4.10pm in the language lab. After three days of complete success, I decided to arrive a few minutes early to get a head-start on things. To my horror, the next person to arrive was the head of modern languages – an old, chalk-haired duffer who looked stunned to find a naked lad in the darkened room muttering, 'I wanted you so much in class today.' Desperate to keep my girl out of trouble, I chose an excuse that I regret to this very day. I told the old fool that I was confused, and had strange feelings for him. No more was said, but I was dumped two days later for another teacher.

Avon calling!

Gent's lubricant horror

A few years ago, I pulled a 'naughty forty'. She didn't need much persuading to accompany me back to my mother's house, where I was living. During the early stages of foreplay, she left me in no doubt as to what she would like me to do to her … I can't explain in full, as I'm led to believe it may still be illegal in this country. I left the bedroom and stumbled to the bathroom without turning on the light, so as not to disturb my mother sleeping in the adjacent room, I returned with a pot of the best lubricant I could find and applied it liberally to the appropriate areas. Ten minutes into my routine, I noticed a distinct chafing that I'd never experienced before. But I saw the job through to the end and was soon kipping soundly. Imagine my horror when I awoke in the morning to discover my manhood looking as if it had been dipped in concrete and my mum's Avon face-mask next to the bed.

Tenting disguised

Lover stuns prospective in-laws

One Sunday my mate Steve and his fiancée drove to the local garden centre with her parents. During the trip, his good lady started touching him up on the back seat and her fingers soon had the desired effect. Once they arrived at the centre, Steve realized that as the car had no back doors, he would have to take great care exiting the vehicle in order to hide his obvious excitement. When his mother-in-law to be opened the door and pulled the seat down he executed a smooth, half-crouching manoeuvre, before turning swiftly and marching off towards the plants. Relieved that he had escaped a potentially embarrassing situation, he was then stunned to hear a familiar voice on the other side of the conifers exclaim: 'Did you see the size of his hard-on, Frank? I thought he was going to have my bloody eye out.'

Rustic lovers

Anglers enjoy free show

Last summer my girlfriend and I spent a glorious day on the banks of a loch in northern Scotland. Having enjoyed our picnic and a couple of bottles of chilled Chardonnay, we both became very horny. I had the bright idea of setting up the tent early for a bit of afternoon sex, and we crawled inside for a long, drawn-out session. We stayed inside for a couple of hours, running through a variety of positions and thoroughly enjoying ourselves in the fresh Scottish air. Eventually I got dressed and climbed out of the tent for a late afternoon ciggie. On my emergence I saw two fishermen sitting in a rowboat at the shore of the loch. I said hello and they smiled at me, waved, and rowed away. I looked back up at the tent and saw that, due to the setting sun, our tent was totally transparent, and the anglers had obviously had a perfect view of my girlfriend and I going through our contortions.

Video exposure

Waitress relieves barman

Years ago, I worked in a hotel during my summer holidays. The place only had one till, and this was shared between the bar and the restaurant. There was a lot of pilfering. As it was used by so many members of staff, it was very hard for the management to find out who had the sticky fingers, so they decided to install a security camera to catch the culprits. At the end of the first session with the new equipment we were all called into the office to watch as our boss fast-forwarded through the tape. This boring task produced no evidence at all, and we were all just about to fall asleep when, on the screen, one of the waitresses, clearly getting a bit carried away with the task of kissing one of the barmen goodnight, dropped to her knees and gave him a very expert blow job – much to our amusement. The video tape still survives to this day, and works perfectly well as a training video for new staff members.

First date horror

One-night stand is off-colour

I was working in Edinburgh as a nightclub manager a few years ago, and one evening a gorgeous girl came up to me and asked me if I would like to go out with her the following night. I couldn't believe my luck and shared my good news with two of the club's bouncers, Steve and Tom. The following night I was changing in the club and getting excited about my big date.

Suddenly Tom and Steve came in, held me down and poured green food colouring all over my bollocks. As I was only minutes away from my date, I let the stuff dry, got dressed and went to meet Jackie. We had a great evening: a meal with some wine, some dancing with plenty of drinks, and she invited me back to her place. We got down to some drunken shagging and I fell asleep a very contented man. I was woken at 7 am by Jackie screaming. She was standing in front of the mirror: her face was green, her tits were green, her hands were green and her thighs were green. She had to take the day off work and never spoke to me again.

Art appreciation

Romantic holiday ruined by sex

Last summer I rented a villa on the Canary Islands with my girlfriend and her parents. It was situated right on the beach front and, one hot evening, the lovely romantic setting had us feeling a little saucy, so the love of my life led me down to the sand for some sexual activity. Things were going great, but as I took her doggy style she looked over her shoulder and grumpily shouted, 'Do me harder, you ginger tosser!'

Devastated, I stopped, and headed back to the house to sleep alone on the sofa. Things got much worse at breakfast however, when her mother haughtily told us that during their evening stroll, a young girl was heard to shout, 'Do me harder, you ginger tosser.' Then suddenly they noticed my bright red barnet. We got back to Blighty, and I was well and truly dumped.

Props poorly chosen

Cowboy attempts clean run

Back in the Sixties, the cult television show for us kids was The Lone Ranger. One of the lads, Barry, received the full outfit for his ninth birthday, and we were all immediately dispatched to find suitable props so that we could join his Lone Ranger gang. Mum had gone to the shops, so I searched through the house until I found some suitable material, and cut two holes in it to make a brilliant mask. Then we galloped off behind Lone Ranger to Dead-Man's Gulch (back of the Co-Op). As we passed through the throngs of shoppers however, I was suddenly whisked off my feet by my furious mother, who spanked me all the way home. Apparently, seeing her five-year-old son charging through the local shopping centre with her sanitary towel tied around his head had played a little on her nerves.

Pet torture

A dog on heat

Visiting my parents for the weekend, I went into the lounge expecting to be pounced upon by my parents' dog, an adorable Yorkshire terrier named Crosby. But the dog remained prostrate on a blanket on the sofa, looking extremely sorry for himself. 'What's up with the dog?' I asked. My father burst out laughing and my mother put down the newspaper she was reading and stormed off, muttering, 'Oh don't start again, Harold!' Dad continued laughing hysterically, then explained:

'At breakfast, your mum decided to spray Crosby with flea spray. She got hold of him, laid him belly up and gave him a good old spray. But, as she was knelt in front of the gas fire, the flea spray ignited like in *Live And Let Die* and set the dog's balls aflame! Crosby sprang up and ran around with his balls on fire! I chased him around the lounge for 40 seconds before I managed to stop him and slap his balls to put the flames out!'

Unfortunately mocked

Father adds insult to injury

While shopping in our local supermarket with my five-year-old son, Jordan, I noticed a young 'differently abled' girl walking through the fresh fruit section with the aid of a pair of tripod crutches. Jordan began staring, so I picked him up and we quickly disappeared off into the aisles. Having bought half the store, I paid for our groceries, then we joined the back of a large queue for lottery tickets. As we waited, the same girl walked past with her entire family in tow – prompting the ever-curious Jordan to tug at my trousers, point at her walking aids and demand, 'What are they for, dad?' Feeling myself going a deep shade of crimson, I gave the girl an embarrassed smile before saying to my lad, 'They're to help the girl walk better, son.' To my horror the 'girl' looked me straight in the eye and bellowed, 'I'm not a girl, I'm a boy!' before storming out. Slowly. Needless to say, I didn't get to play the lottery that weekend.

Training trauma

Daughter paints father

After a pretty horrendous training weekend with the Royal Marines Reserves, I came home and fell asleep on the sofa – only to wake up to a tingling sensation in my feet. My young daughter had taken my shoes and socks off. I went back to my well-deserved kip.

The next morning, I found out what my daughter had done, but by then it was too late to do anything about it. I just made a mental note to deal with her later. At the camp, five minutes into a run with the lads and our instructor, I twisted my ankle in a pothole and was carried off to sickbay. All gathered round to see if it was a juicy injury (sick bastards, these marine types). Then the doc took off my sock. To my – and everyone else's – horror, my toe nails were painted with pink Barbie doll nail varnish! And did they believe my story? Did they fuck!

Dumb childhood antic

Nipper sees stars

When I was a child, friends and I would play on the railway line just outside our town. We would wave to drivers and passengers and occasionally place an ear on the line to see if we could hear a train approaching. One day I decided to listen, and squatted down, took hold of the track and put my ear against it. There was a loud bang, a bright flash and I landed, rather stunned, in a bush ten feet away. I'd forgotten that there were three lines with one carrying the electric current. Presumably my rubber-soled plimsolls and both hands making simultaneous contact had saved my life. The short-term effects were some faint burns down the inside of my arms and legs. Longer term was the mixture of awe and derision with which I was treated by my peers. And of course I never told my mother – she would have killed me.

Show-off bounced

Smitten child given shock

When I was eight I had a girlfriend called Antoinette. I thought we would last forever, until I saw her snogging a boy called Ross in the playground after school. I was gutted, but decided to try and win her back. My plan was to impress her with my football skills, so one afternoon I stood outside her house and began a lengthy session of 'keepy-ups'. Eventually she came to the window to watch, so I started getting a little cockier, and eventually lost control of the ball. She smiled, I waved, turned to get the ball, and got run over by a Ford Sierra. I remember her scream as I bounced off the bonnet and somersaulted off down the street. I spent the entire Easter holiday in traction, and never spoke to her again.

Wild beast

Child finds unlikely toy

Not so long ago, I agreed to help my girlfriend babysit her nine-year-old niece at her sister's house, knowing a decent shag would be my reward. Before long – with the brat safely tucked away – the couch became my jungle of love as I unveiled my surprise – a novelty elephant posing-pouch. With my glistening little chap fitting the trunk, and my sweaty balls swinging sweetly in its cheeks, I danced my arse off like a horny Zulu, all to the desired effect: the sopping jizz-filled pouch was finally abandoned and we embarked on a humping safari. In the morning, long after we had departed, my lover's sister gasped in horror as her daughter shook her awake and proudly said: 'Mummy, look at my new mask.'

Sporting snacks

Fat skier eats for two

When I was 10 years old I went on a primary school skiing trip to Austria. At the time I was a very fat and very short little boy, and my mum had elected to dress me in tight white polo neck jumpers, and emerald green, arse-hugging ski pants, which only served to emphasis my porcine features. Towards the end of an afternoon on the slopes, my mate Mark and I snuck off to a café, popped our skis on the rack, and headed inside. Mark asked me to get him a king-size chocolate bar while he went to the loo. I bought the food, but when Mark had failed to return after five minutes, I began to eye his share of the grub hungrily.

Eventually I succumbed to temptation but just as I began to nibble at the top of the choccy feast, a group of Englishmen strolled in and stopped to stare at me. I can only assume they thought I was a local and couldn't speak English, as one nudged his mate and said, 'I bet that fat twat is going to eat the lot.' And I did.

Hangover horror

Fetch the retch rover

After getting violently pissed to celebrate my friend's birthday, he and I staggered back to his parents' house to crash out. I was directed to a room which was full of ladders and without lights, so getting to the bathroom was going to be difficult. As the room started spinning I decided that it would be best to puke on the floor and clean it up in the morning.

According to plan, I awoke early but then reality reared its ugly head. A great spray of puke had gone over his mother's clothes and had liberally covered the bed. Have you ever tried removing dried vomit from the channels in corduroys? Keeping a cool head I scraped all the spew into a pillow case with a birthday card, deposited it in the neighbour's garden and put the sheets and clothes back in the washing machine.

Later, while having breakfast with the family, an eerie scratching came from the door. It swung open to reveal their dog with a multicoloured pungent pillow case swinging from its mouth.

Weird love triangle

Faithful hound joins in

One night, feeling amorous, I convinced my girlfriend to don a figure-hugging basque and black fishnet stockings. She duly obliged and we soon got down to business. To get the best view of her perfectly-formed mesh-covered legs, I suggested we do it 'doggy fashion' over her favourite armchair. We were indulging in some frantic sex when I realized my right leg was too close to her two-bar electric fire. But I was too near the point of no return to change position, so instead I began to yelp involuntarily, which my girlfriend took as a signal of my increasing ecstasy. She started moaning and yelping in a similar fashion, and the sideways jerks I made to distance myself from the heat only made her more enthusiastic. Then I had an even stranger sensation. Just as I was about to come, her labrador stuck its cold, wet nose right up my arse.

My body spasmed in every direction – with shock and pain – while my girlfriend was in ecstasy. I never told her about our third party!

Student politics

Steroidal bunnies set loose

While I was a student, I became mixed up in left-wing politics. Part of my initiation was to demonstrate my dedication to the protection of a group of animals which were being cruelly practised upon in the labs of the local university biology department. Some of the beasts really were being appallingly treated: skin was shaved from little puppies so that after shave could be tested; mice were force-fed with drugs; and rabbits were jacked up with steroids – all in the name of research. One night a gang of like-minded mini-revolutionaries and I decided to set free the rabbits – which happened to be the most accessible animals, as they were kept in hutches which backed onto the fields at the edge of town. We donned our balaclavas and black donkey jackets and crept down to the labs.

Nobody was about, so we bolt-cropped the locks and opened the hatch doors onto the fields, and freedom. Naturally, we didn't stick around to watch the results of our handiwork. The following day at lectures we heard we had been successful: the rabbits had all got out. Unfortunately, we hadn't considered their steroidal history. It turns out that 35 rabbits made a grab for freedom – animals that weighed, on average, just over 25lb each. Tragically, the rabbits had all been unnaturally thirsty due to steroid dehydration, and the first source of water they had come across was the cess-pipe of the local cereal factory. The poor bunnies had lapped at the fetid water until dead, and the local newspaper described the eerie scene the following morning as a 'floating, fluffy armada of death'.

Damp feline

Pussy gets soaking

Some years ago I went to my cousin's engagement party in Greenwich, where the toilet was an outhouse in the back yard. When I needed to relieve myself, there was a long queue, so I decided to do it in the fish pond. In my haste I didn't realize that my aunt's cat was sitting at the water's edge, and the poor thing got covered. Shortly afterwards my aunt entered the garden and picked up the cat. While stroking it she said: 'The cat's all wet!' 'Oh,' I said, 'she must have fallen in the pond.'

Bath-tub accident

Younger brother receives marble

When I was a lot younger – just nine years old, to be exact – the Sunday evening rituals always included a weekly bath. My younger brother, Nigel, and I used to enjoy sharing a tub, and our mother would counsel us on the damage small objects could cause. Even though we had been warned, it didn't stop us sneaking model soldiers, bricks of Lego and countless other small objects into the bathroom to play with in the steaming water.

One of our favourite bath-time toys was a large, purple, clear glass marble. One Sunday evening my brother and I were playing our soapy games, as usual, when a terrible accident occurred. My younger brother, having stood up to 'dive bomb' some of the floating plastic soldiers with pieces of Lego, sat down with a splash, having successfully taken out three men. Nigel also sat down with a high-pitched scream, which drove me to have a fit of hysterical laughter, not knowing why he was causing such a fuss. The large purple marble, lurking unseen like a mine at the bottom of the soapy water, had been forced up my poor brother's brown star.

Consequently, poor Nigel spent a long, drawn-out evening face down on the kitchen table, having the glass marble removed with the aid of the ends of two teaspoons and a liberal amount of olive oil.

Helpful brochure

Eagerness proves downfall

During my penultimate year of school, pupils were required to attend a careers seminar to help fashion a plan for our futures. Being an active chap, I decided to attend the lecture on the sports industry. Our speaker was a local entrepreneur who had formed a successful sports agency and, having been issued a copy of the company prospectus, I noticed that on the second page there was a picture of him with Colin Montgomerie, the rather rotund, red-faced Scottish golfer. Such a lucrative client must have proven invaluable to the company and, keen to make an impression, I saw it as an ideal point to bring up at the question and answer session. Right on cue, at the end of a somewhat tedious speech, I thrust my hand in the air and made my point to the speaker, who simply stared at me, totally bemused. 'See,' I began, holding the prospectus in the air for all to see. 'Colin Montgomerie.' Looking closely at the page, the entrepreneur made eye-contact and said, 'That, young man, is my wife and I.' Needless to say, my summer job at the company never materialized.

Flatulent camel

Beast causes ruckus

On holiday in Egypt, my mates and I realized that after a week hanging around the bars of Cairo, we should do the decent thing and visit the pyramids – and have a monkey about on the camels. We had a root around the ruins before paying one of the camel handlers a few pence and clambering aboard a bundle of bored-looking beasts. Almost immediately, my camel started farting – much to the amusement of my mates, and also a young American couple, whose porky little toddler found it especially hilarious. Predictably, the Egyptian camel owner went to town with the gag, pointing at me every time the mangy animal let rip, and sharing a smile with the Americans, who he was obviously tapping up for his next trip. For five long minutes, my mates and I were led around like idiots, the camel parping merrily away all the time. Just as I was getting off the beast, the American couple swaggered over and started haggling with the owner, when the camel opened its voluminous bowels straight onto the head of their over-fed child, spattering him with hard, lumpy shit. Suddenly, without warning, the kid's father lunged at me and gave me a hard thump on the arm, as if I was responsible, before joining his fretting wife, busy clearing poo from the mewling brat's face. Outraged but confused, all I could think of doing was picking up a turd and flinging it at the trio, which I did – before running off into a big crowd of tourists.

Surfing horror

Drunk messes up foot

The Christmas before last I was in a pub being drunk and obnoxious, and was thrown out. Leaving the pub, I saw a huge tanker lorry driving very slowly up the narrow street, and thought I would have some fun. I jogged up behind the lorry and jumped onto the small ladder on the back, then got on the roof and tried a bit of 'urban surfing'. All was going well until the lorry suddenly sped up, and before I knew it I was lying on the roof as the thing pulled onto a dual carriageway. I went to the back of the lorry and climbed down the ladder, but the road was moving past very, very fast. Panicking, I decided I could jump off and simply manage to run along the road really quickly.

The next few hours are a blur. Apparently a car ran over my foot, which was broken in six places, and I got a blood clot on my big toe. Besides this, I suffered bruising and contusions. Sadly, my toe went black and scummy. Three months later, when pulling on my jeans, I snagged the manky toe, and the whole bloody thing fell off. Thankfully, I can now walk again, but I don't do urban surfing anymore.

Flour fiasco

Chef gets blocked

As any professional cook will tell you, long hours spent in front of the stoves can result in the condition we call Chef's Arse – where your ring becomes red-raw and sitting down is difficult, to say the least. The best remedy is a good handful of cornflour, up and around the offending area. I was halfway through a double-shift when Chef's Arse last struck. The chafing was unbearable, so, unable to locate the cornflour, I took a packet of plain flour into the loo, gratefully slathered it over my hairy arse, and finished my shift, pain-free. Next morning, I launched into my usual routine: black coffee, ciggy, followed by turd time – so I entered the loo, dropped my trousers and went for the big squeeze. My scream woke the entire house. My arse-spiders had meshed with the flour and sweat to create a near-impenetrable, hairy net over my crack, through which I'd attempted to crimp off a length.

Hole puncher

Man gets nuts in a twist

While working in a large furniture showroom, I was asked by the manager to lift a remarkably heavy worktop. Seeing me struggle, a workmate who shall remain nameless, and was working nearby drilling holes into doors – rushed over to help. Needing to use both hands, he popped the cordless drill into the waistband of his jeans, and leaned down to get a decent grip.

As he did so, his belt pulled on the trigger, and the drill spun into action, promptly wrapping his scrotum round the 3-inch drill bit. We thought he was screaming loudly at that point, but when we were then forced to switch the thing into reverse to unwrap his squashed goolies, he very nearly burst our eardrums.

When he finally returned to work, he had three stitches
and a comedy John Wayne walk.

Sofa sex shock

Lover loses old fella

My girlfriend and I had been together for four months when we decided, at last, to consummate our relationship. I'm not afraid to admit that I was nervous – I wanted our first time together to be special. In short, I wanted to prove that I was an insatiable sex god. We had the house to ourselves and began to get closer in the living room. Heavy petting, panting and foreplay ensued, and I pushed forward. But instead of getting that joyous, warm sensation, my willy was hit by a rough jolt which caused immense pain.

On top of that, I was getting a strange feeling which can only be compared to a cocktail stick wiggling about in a bucket. After five minutes of very little pleasure and occasional agonizing stabs, I gave up and looked down, expecting to see my willy in tatters. Fortunately, I was still intact, but I found I had been shagging the gap between the cushions on the sofa. Instead of hitting her G-spot, I hit a metal spring and a copy of *Reader's Digest*.

Bloody sex

Bellybutton agony

I was once having a relationship with a girl who decided to get her bellybutton pierced. I was all for this, and was even more up for it when I saw how sexy it made her stomach look. I was so turned on, in fact, that we got down to some heavy petting, which was going along swimmingly until she decided to pull my jeans down for some more hardcore action. Somehow, in the heat of the moment, the button on my jeans got caught up in her bellybutton ring. And as she tugged my jeans she ripped down hard on the ring. Blood squirted from her stomach and she let out a howl. I quickly held a towel to the wound, hoping it was just a slight scratch. But when we pulled back the bloodsoaked towel we were horrified to find my girl's bellybutton, complete with ring, hanging at the end of a strip of skin. Instead of spending the summer with a beautifully exposed midriff my girlfriend ended up covering up a stitched wound, which turned into a hideous scar.

Drama down under

Driver faces a hard time

Some years ago my tank squadron was engaged in training exercises in the northern outback of Australia. We covered huge expanses of hot and hostile territory with a driver nicknamed Horse. After one very long drive, he stopped our truck, complaining that his face was burnt and he needed a break. Remembering a choice purchase during our last visit to town, I offered him a bowl filled with something that looked like Germolene to soothe his burn. Horse smeared it liberally all over his face. Within minutes, the poor bloke's head had ballooned up to twice its size, sending him careering off into the outback, followed by a swarm of red flying ants that were smitten by the smell of the freshly applied cream. Everybody stood with their mouths open as I admitted that Horse was running around like an idiot with 'Sammy Stay Hard' erection cream all over his face. He hasn't retaliated yet, but after-sun on my cock wouldn't seem nearly as bad.

Welsh accident

River plunge horror

During my early teenage years, a bunch of mates and I would bike several miles to a river near Llangollen in north Wales. Here we had constructed a rope swing fairly high up on the bank, tied to the branch of a tree. We would swing out over the river and drop into the dark, still waters below – at times we must have reached a height of a good 20ft before letting go of the rope. Anyway, the years rolled by, and in May this year we went back to the area for a few beers near our old haunt. The day was hot and dusty, so we decided to nip down to the rope for a dip. We staggered along the riverbank, and before long one of my mates spotted an old rope swinging in the breeze.

He tore off his clothes and ran at the rope, getting a great swing out over the river, and let go a good 25ft above the surface. To our horror, my mate splashed into just three feet of water and let out an horrific scream. It was the wrong place. He ended up with two broken ankles.

Pylon shocker

Son hit by worried father

A lad I know works on the oil rigs, on a two-weeks-on, two-weeks-off rota, and whenever he's home he always calls in on his old Dad to see if any jobs need doing. On this one occasion, his Dad had asked him to weed the end of the garden so, spade in hand, he set about the task. After a short while, he became aware of a small stone in his boot, which he struggled to dislodge. This proved more and more difficult as the stone worked its way further into his boot, so he leant on the leg of a nearby electricity pylon to try to shake it out. At this point, his Dad, who was washing up, glanced out of the kitchen window to see his son 'stuck' to the pylon, shaking his leg like crazy.

Thinking the worst, the old man ran out of the house, picked up a spade and twatted his son with all his might in an attempt to break the 'current'. Instead, all he succeeded in breaking was his poor son's arm.

Unsafe sex

Condom instructions misread

When I was a lad I joined a Youth Training Scheme, and one week we were taken on an Outward Bound course in the Brecon Beacons. Once there we found, to our dismay, that the girls were split from the lads for our sleeping arrangements. Naturally, the next week was spent sneaking to and fro, and generally getting together at night was the prime concern of us all. But my mate Paul was very inexperienced with girls, and one evening he asked me about condoms. I told him to make sure he covered it all up because he didn't want the horror of crabs. Anyway, this one night we were all in the girls' dorm, quietly trying to have our shags, when a terrible piercing scream came from one of the beds. Out jumped Paul, who had a look of excruciating pain on his face: the stupid idiot had pulled the condom open and snapped it over not just his penis but also his scrotum. The tightened johnny not only caused awful pain in his nuts but also scooped a healthy bunch of pubic hair, causing agony to my naive friend.

Freak injury

Good intentions cripple player

When I was studying in Ireland, I took up rugby. As my first season wore on, the lads and I were eventually scheduled to play a team which had quite a reputation for violent play. Considering that we weren't the most talented outfit to have ever taken the field, we decided to accept the challenge with a 'do or die' attitude, hoping things would eventually swing our way. They didn't, and to make matters worse our star player, Alan, dislocated his hip after a particularly ferocious tackle. He was clearly in a lot of pain, so we all stood back to watch the medic who, in one swift movement, managed to slot the hip back into its socket. Then Alan began a long, blood-curdling scream. To our horror, we realized that one of his testicles had also been jammed into the socket, and was now firmly held in place by the hip. Incidentally, Alan managed to rip a vocal chord with his screaming.

Chopping horror

Engineer leaves lover with small tip

A few years ago I was working on a YTS engineering course and I had a nasty accident, chopping the end off my right index finger with a milling machine. I was rushed to hospital where, luckily, they managed to sew my severed finger back on again. After several weeks, my bandages were removed and I was horrified to find the finger hadn't healed properly, and was still very scabby. It was a nasty sight, but the nurse assured me this was quite normal, and all would be well within a few weeks.

Anyway, two weeks later I was indulging in some vigorous 'finger sex' with my girlfriend after the annual Judo Club Disco. When I'd finished pleasuring the lucky girl I was horrified to find that the end of my finger was missing! After a vigorous body search we eventually found the offending stub, and I'm happy to say my fingers are now all in one piece.

Ironing board mishap

Paralytic man gets interesting scar

One afternoon, a friend had a few problems that required discussion over a few pints in the local pub. One thing led to another and before I realized the time, my friend and I had sunk one too many and staggered home. I was living in student accommodation at the time so the house was in a right state – shite everywhere – including the ironing board and iron just outside my room. Expecting my girlfriend to pick me up in an hour or so, I headed off to iron a shirt, but a tremendous fatigue entered my body and I thought, 'Well OK, just a quick lie down'. Six hours later I was woken by the telephone ringing. I crashed out of my room, knowing I was horribly late, at exactly the same time as one of my house mates picked up the phone and shouted to me that it was my girlfriend. To this day, I cannot explain or comprehend why I did what I did, but, on hearing my mate, I grabbed the iron thinking it was the telephone and felt it sizzle my cheek as I held it up to my ear. It had been on for six hours and by this stage it compared to the heat generated at the core of the earth. I looked in the mirror and saw V shaped indentations burnt onto my cheek. You could even see the holes where the steam comes out. The public humiliation lasted almost as long as the scar.

Batteries included

Couch potato feels the heat

One Christmas, about seven years ago, I was lying in bed in my parents' house watching TV. When I tried to change channel, I discovered that the remote wasn't working, and despite whacking it on the bedside table, it refused to come to life. It was bloody cold, so I took the batteries out and popped them under the pillow to warm some life into them. Five minutes later, still nothing, so I put them in the warmest place I knew – right between my buttocks. Then I realized that the batteries were leaking – the pain was incredible, and I ran to the bathroom. Keeping one leg on the floor, I lifted the other up into the sink, and furiously splashed water onto my burning starfish. It was then I realized I wasn't alone. My father had been woken by my groans, and was standing behind me with an extremely stern expression. Eventually he accepted my explanation, but he rarely lets me near the remote when I'm at home now.

Morning shaving incident

The man who licked his razor

One morning, after staggering bleary-eyed from the shower, a glance in the mirror confirmed I needed a shave. As I had little faith in my hand-to-eye coordination so early on in the day, a wet shave was out of the question. I grabbed the electric shaver and switched it on. I don't remember which thoughts had crept into my semi-conscious mind, but they certainly had nothing to do with the job in hand. I stood looking at the razor, feeling its vibrations in my hand and listening to the hypnotic hum. Then I inexplicably brought it slowly towards my face and licked it.

I stood motionless, transfixed by pain and mesmerized by my sheer stupidity, watching droplets of deep red blood rapidly appear and spread from the tiny grazes across the tip of my tongue. The bathroom mirror misted up once more. I was late for work.

Thick fog

Care worker hospitalizes wards

Working as a care assistant, I was recently 'volunteered' to supervise a group of unruly kids on a canal barge trip. I soon understood why my work colleagues were so keen to stay in the office: four hours of navigating around dead dogs and shopping trolleys while attempting to control a load of screaming, hyperactive children. But suddenly, near the halfway mark, we hit a stretch of the canal blanketed by thick, odd, yellowish fog, apparently emanating from a house on the bank. There was nothing else for it: inspired by boredom and exasperation, I grabbed the set of bongos I kept below deck and sat cross-legged on the bow. As the barge drifted into the sepia gloom, I began to strike a tribal beat – and, grinning wildly, the kids began to dance. It was like something out of *Apocalypse Now*. We were still chuckling, in fact, when we got home. And then we were told there'd been a fire at a local chemical refinery, and one of the tanks had leaked toxic, sulphurous fumes across the area. With the noise of the engine, we hadn't heard local radio reports cautioning people to stay indoors. Three of the children had to spend the night in casualty before getting the all-clear, and I was promptly fired.

Copper caught short

Plod showers unfortunate corpse

I'm a police officer, and a few years ago I was out on night patrol with my shift partner, Dave. The sarge radioed us and explained that there had been a death at a nearby top-floor flat, and that he would meet us there. When we arrived we found an old dear, completely dead, with her head resting on the toilet seat – tragically, she had passed away while attempting to vomit. I went into the living room and began filling out the forms, when the sarge suddenly got another call, and shot off, taking Dave with him. Ten minutes later I had finished the forms, and now had a more pressing problem – I was desperate for a pee, and couldn't use her sink as it was full of washing. I lasted about an hour-and-a-half before I could take no more. Straddling the old woman, I let rip; using all my skill to keep the golden stream about three inches from her wrinkled face. At that moment the sarge walked in, followed by Dave, two undertakers and the woman's middle-aged daughter.

To round things off, I zipped up so quickly that the daughter saw me splash warm piss dribble all over her dead mother's head.

Student scorched

Scally dabbles with fire

During my final year at university I lived in a student house with a Scouser and other assorted drunken yobs, where we had a tradition: whoever lasted longest on the piss would set off the smoke alarm on their return home. So it came as no surprise at 3am one morning to be woken by an alarm. Placing a pillow over my head, I waited for the triumphant drinker to reset the alarm and head off for bed.

However, after ten minutes it became obvious that something was different, as a girl's screams penetrated the electronic wail. I tumbled out of my pit and followed the screams to the Scouser's room, where I was greeted by the sight of his bird jumping up and down on the bed, half naked, waving a sheet at the smoke alarm – while the Scally ran about with his dressing gown on fire. It turned out that when his girlfriend had spurned his offer of a night of lurve, he'd waited till she was asleep then, bored, started lighting his own farts – until he produced such a ripper that he set his nightwear on fire. After extinguishing the flames, we of course called him 'Ring of Fire' for the rest of his university life – a fact I shall remind him of when I attend his wedding this summer.

Karate cock-up

Macho man's shortcomings

In the middle of an all-day drinking binge with a friend of mine – who happened to be a karate instructor – we decided to pay a visit to a house where several of our friends lived, to stretch the day's fun as far as possible. Then all of us went into town to a pub, where, with the usual brash bravado, play-fights started to develop. My friend, who was very much the worse for wear, then decided to challenge everyone to a karate battle. Naturally, everybody declined, which led to the drunken martial arts instructor becoming more and more agitated. He loudly proclaimed that he could whip anyone with just his little finger, which was met with howls of derision.

He next shouted that he could beat everyone with his ear, his eye and, finally, with his cock. When this final bullshit claim produced no takers, he unzipped his jeans, pulled out his flaccid johnson and began waving it in the air shouting, 'I could have you with this!' What he hadn't noticed was that the window – which made up one side of the pub – had filled with dozens of curious on-lookers, all of whom were loudly applauding his humiliating performance. To this day, he's still known in town as 'Maggot'.

Filthy cocktail

Wounded man's sick drink

At a college party several months ago, I found myself
in the kitchen, drunk, and messing about with a knife.
My friend and I were taking turns spinning the knife in
the air and trying to catch it by its handle as it came
down. Naturally, after several drunken attempts I
missed the handle and grabbed the knife by the blade,
causing a really deep gash in my finger. In our pissed
state, my friend and I deemed the wound not serious
enough for a trip to the hospital, and decided to drain
my blood into a glass before attending to the wound.
We did this successfully, managing to get about a third
of a glassful of blood, which we topped up with vodka,
Worcestershire Sauce and a few drops of Tabasco. We

gave the drink a swirl, and decided to present it to the next person to walk into the kitchen. I would just like to take this opportunity to say to my mate Laney: that's the most authentic Bloody Mary you'll ever have.

Manmade cocktail

Jilted lover gets dousing

Having been recently dumped by my girlfriend, my mates decided that I needed cheering up and dragged me down the local nightclub. I was having a brilliant time, when the ex suddenly walked in with her new boyfriend in tow. Spotting me, the pair performed a victory snog right in front of me, before heading for the bar. Determined to dish out a suitable punishment, I nipped to the toilet where, with the help of several revellers, I filled a pint glass with warm pee, and headed out to the bar where they were standing. My plan was to launch the pint over my shoulder catching them square in the face with piss, but as my arm shot up, I noticed that they were watching my every move.

Panicking, I tried to stop my arm, but succeeded only in pouring the frothy liquid straight over my head and down my back. They laughed so much, one of the bouncers brought over some chairs, shortly before throwing me out.

Fatal attraction

Stray punch floors pest

Unwanted attention is frustrating at the best of times, but during the three years of your life when you're supposed to be nobbing yourself lame, it's positively infuriating. At university I was unlucky enough to attract the attention of the most irritating girl on campus. She was fat, noisy, always stuck her nose in where it didn't belong, and followed me around with a look of puppy dog adoration on her face no matter how often I told her to go away. After several months of this style cramping I'd had enough, and I told anyone who cared to listen that I was sick of her and I was going to put a stop to her evil ways. One night in the bar I was drunkenly ranting to some friends about what a cow she was when, unseen to me, she sat down just behind me. I had become highly animated by this point and told everyone that I would like to knock her out. I illustrated this by swinging a giant haymaker. Unfortunately, I swung right round and lamped the girl in the face, knocking her clean out of her seat, and splattering her face with blood. Everybody assumed I'd done it deliberately and for months I was labelled as a woman-beater, while she became very popular as the innocent victim.

Reveller repulsed

Greenie finds new home

During the Christmas party season in London, every late-night tube home is packed with drunks – which is how I found myself opposite a smartly dressed middle-aged woman who must have had one too many and fallen asleep. Sitting beside her was a scruffy old wino who was drifting in and out of consciousness and swaying all over the place, finally slumping with his head inches above the woman's arm. A stream of green, lumpy mucus then began to stream out of the old lush's mouth, falling into a neat pile on the woman's arm, until the train bumped into a station and the old man slumped in the other direction. The woman jerked awake, and

as her eyes opened she caught sight of the green
slime on her sleeve. Before my astonished eyes,
assuming it was her own, she greedily gobbled up
the old man's mucus.

Nightmare on 16th green

Winning golfer humiliated

Needing a crap on the way home from a day-time drinking session with some college friends, I managed to persuade my boozing buddies to take a short-cut across the golf course so I could have a dump on their private, well-manicured lawns. However, much to the amusement of my mates, I decided to squat over the hole on the 16th green and let a perfect turd slip into the cup. We then retired to the safety of the trees as a group of players appeared on the horizon. They played up to the green, and met with our polite applause as they neared the hole and their final putts. Finally, the star player, with much posturing, sank his putt, and strutted over to the hole to smugly retrieve his winning ball. Then everything seemed to go into slow motion as he knelt down, still grinning at the crowd, lowered his hand into the hole and slowly withdrew his ball. As he looked down, his face became confused, then contorted, as he realized that his hand, and his ball, were speckled with smudges of shit. He didn't even have the decency to yell 'Fore!' as he threw caution to the wind and launched the brown-stained projectile at the cackling drunks who were by now legging it through the rough.

Golden showers

Mates get unwelcome drenching

One hot day last year I went to an all-day music festival with a bunch of mates. Because of the enormous crowd it took ages to fight our way to the front for the best view. Unfortunately, because we had spent the entire morning drinking, by the time we were in pole position we were all desperate for a pee.

Unwilling to lose our hard-won vantage point we were resigned to spending the next few hours in agony, until one bright spark realized that we could piss into our now empty plastic beer glasses and then drop them over the other side of the crowd barrier. Bladders now emptied, we relaxed to enjoy the bands. Unluckily for us, as the sun grew hotter the security guards began to work their way along the barrier, throwing pints of water onto the parched crowd. Far too late for us to escape we realized that this water was also in plastic pint glasses, placed strategically behind the crowd barrier. We stood helpless and unable to move as the bouncers got to where we were and threw seven pints of warm, fresh piss all over us.

Night bus incident

Sneaky drunk caught out

A few months ago, having been out for a few drinks with some friends, I decided to catch the bus home. As I strolled to the bus stop I saw the bus coming – there's only one an hour at that time of night – and dashed to catch it. Luckily the driver waited for me and I boarded the bus. I sat down in a seat next to a group of fairly drunk girls, and before long I was desperate for a pee. There was no way I was getting off and waiting another hour for a bus, so I tried to think of other things. The girls got talking to me and I found myself in the odd position of having to control my bladder while I was being chatted up. Every bump, corner and sudden stop was a nightmare as I strained to control my bladder. Finally, I had a bright idea. I pulled out my fags and made my way to the top deck. Luck! Nobody was up there, so had a long, joyous pee, taking care to put my jacket over the driver's spy-mirror. I zipped up and went downstairs, only to be sworn at, pushed and hit by the previously friendly girls. What I didn't know was that there were drains on the top deck, and my pee had gone down one and back in the sliding window – all over the girls.

Water-gun pranks

Party-goer ingests urine

On Christmas Day in 1995, I was lucky enough to find myself on the other side of the world, in Sydney, Australia. Twenty-five or so close friends and I were enjoying a marvellous barbecue in the sweltering weather, complete with cold beers and plenty of party games. One girl, Liz, who had drunk enough Castlemaine XXXX to stun the Wallabies, amused herself for several hours by running around with a high-powered water rifle, and took great delight in shooting powerful jets of water at unsuspecting friends. This was quite funny for an hour or two, but pretty soon people began to get a bit tired of having their beer and backs watered down every five minutes. Eventually I snatched the watergun off her, leaving her to find some other form of amusement.

I then took the rifle into the khazi and filled it with piss. Back at the barbie, I set about finding the original shooter, who, when I tracked her down, proved to be a good sport. Instead of running away she simply lay down on the grass, laughing. She urged me to 'fill her up' and opened her mouth. Needless to say, I complied, and directed a hot, high-powered jet of pee straight into her wide open mouth. Revenge has perhaps never been sweeter, although Liz left the following day for Tasmania.

Toe trouble

Camper's 'bath'

Back in the mid-Nineties I was asked to go camping by mates, sharing a tent with my girlfriend. We happy campers had a great first night, drinking copiously around the fire in a field in the middle of nowhere. Once we'd retired to my tent, my girlfriend got the horn, and after drunkenly undressing we were soon at it like rabbits, before dropping off into a booze-fuelled sleep. Naturally, I awoke a few hours later dying for a piss, so wandered out into the darkness to take a leak. On my return I found my girl awake and ready to go again – and as that ginger sponger Fergie was all over the papers at the time, she treated me to five minutes of toe-sucking. Next morning we awoke to a

dreadful smell, prompting my girlfriend to quit the
tent in search of breakfast. I then peeled back the
sleeping bag-to find both my feet encrusted in dried
cow-shit from my small-hours ramble. Except, of
course, the one big toe my missus had lovingly
caressed the night before.

Lucrative sickie

Skiver hits paydirt

A couple of years ago me and my flatmate worked for a large company organizing staff incentives, to which we invariably managed to invite ourselves. One such freebie involved taking 30 wage-slaves to a restaurant in London's Chinatown one Friday night. Due to the amount of alcohol I'd previously consumed I couldn't face any Chinese food, but nevertheless carried on drinking until I could hardly walk. The rest of the weekend consisted of hair of the dog, while my mate put his sickness and diarrhoea down to too much wine – but come Monday he was still doubled up in pain. I phoned work on his behalf, when my boss told me that 24 of the people who'd been out that evening had also called in with food poisoning, so naturally I jumped on the bandwagon and, hungover, claimed a couple of sick days myself. I left the company a year later, but three months ago I received a letter from my old employers stating that the Chinese restaurant had admitted responsibility for the food poisoning, and due to the distress were enclosing a cheque for £1,027.50. Now, every time I look at my new dining table and chairs, I happily recall the most profitable hangover I've ever had.

Hooker chunders

Player struck by own mess

Several years ago my rugby team went on its annual coach tour of France. Our hooker at the time was notorious for his excessive booze intake, and by the time we reached Dover, he was ready to burst – which he promptly did, puking up his ring into an empty burger bag. Drunk and weak, he then shoved it up into the skylight and went to sleep. Mercifully, we travelled 120km across France without further incident. When the coach arrived at our town, a small Renault cut us up at the lights, causing the bus driver to slam on the brakes. At that moment our hooker was walking back up the bus and was suddenly catapulted headlong down the aisle. The putrid, freezing carton of sick shot out of its resting place and twatted him straight in the face, exploding on impact. To cap things off, the stench caused another nine hardened players to puke into their laps.

Light bulb craze

Experiment proves contagious

A few weeks ago, after a mind-melting Saturday night on the town, my mates and I headed home for a few vodka nightcaps. After sinking the best part of a bottle, one of the chaps suddenly informed us that if you force a light bulb into your mouth, its particular size and shape apparently forces your jaw to lock. Obviously one of us had to put this theory to the test, and sure enough, within 20 minutes, the four of us were in a taxi on our way to hospital to have a light bulb removed from a locked jaw. After queuing for several hours, we were finally seen by a sympathetic doctor who unscrewed the metal part of the bulb, inserted a small cloth and carefully smashed the glass. Fortunately, other than a sore mouth, my mate wasn't injured, so we headed for home. Just as we were leaving however, a sheepish-looking man walked in with a light bulb wedged in his mouth. It was none other than the same taxi driver who had driven us to the hospital four hours earlier.

Fire fighter

Have-a-go hero gets it wrong

In the summer of 1993, my friend – whom I'll refer to only as Corky – was considering applying to join the fire service. I was in the pub one night with Corky when a girl ran in shouting that there was a burning car outside. Corky, by now in a drunken stupor, seized his chance of gaining firefighting credentials and ran out to assess the situation. Through the plumes of smoke, Corky could just make out a figure slumped against the steering wheel. Ignoring the advice of boozed-up onlookers, he ran to the blazing car, opened the door and attempted to extract the driver. Suddenly, a fire engine arrived: two real firemen jumped out and struggled to remove my choking friend from the wreck. Corky was treated for smoke inhalation and second-degree burns, and was whisked off, unconscious, to the local hospital. Two hours later, he came round, expecting a hero's reception – only to discover that the 'body' was the driver's seat slumped forward, with a furry seat cover hanging from the 'head'.

Trainee drinker's error

Two men in a bed

A few years ago, my main goal in life was to improve my drinking capacity. One evening, I had perhaps taken a little too much alcohol on board, and I was frankly paralytic. Bedtime that night at my girlfriend's place was a frosty affair. During the night nature called and I went to the bathroom, an achievement in itself. I kept the light off in the bedroom and carefully felt the bed to avoid crushing my girlfriend as I got back in. Barely had I made myself comfortable than the bedroom door opened and a shaft of light fell across the bed from the hallway. I looked up to see my girlfriend standing in the doorway with a look of total horror on her face. Not half as horrified as her 16-

year-old brother did, though, crushed up against the wall after I had inadvertently staggered into the wrong bedroom and climbed into his bed! Needless to say, the relationship did not last long after that little gem.

Photo blunder

Drunk men exposed

Following a fairly heavy night on the booze, my friend Alex and I made our way to the station to catch our train home. Feeling pissed and merry, we decided to kill the 15 minutes' wait for our train by mucking about in the passport photo booth. We stuck our two quid in the machine, struck a variety of hilarious poses, then fell out and waited for the results of our work. Unfortunately, while we were waiting, my female boss came up and started a conversation. She was getting the same train as us, and stood chatting as the photo booth made ominous rumblings. Then our photos dropped out. She has never mentioned the episode at work, but I often wonder what she thought of the four pictures of me and Alex waving our todgers at the camera lens, and I still get the odd grin from other female members of staff.

Telephone error

Student bores his girlfriend

Like many a feckless student, I recently spent most of my grant cheque in a single night's drinking at the Student Union. Not being a complete idiot I managed to stagger back to my room for some well-earned sleep in the early hours of the morning. I drank a pint of water and lay down on the bed. Naturally the whole room started swimming, so I stood up to try to work out how to kill some time to get rid of the dizziness. I decided to give my girlfriend a call. This was no simple matter as she was on her year out in India, I had no money, and my phone only took incoming calls. Remembering that my parents had said I could use their chargecard for emergency calls, I decided to put it to use. After several unsuccessful attempts I actually managed to get through and proceeded to have a drunken argument with my highly annoyed girlfriend, who quite rightly pointed out what a wanker and a bore I was. At this I terminated the call, staggered back to bed and crashed out. In the afternoon I woke up and saw the phone was off the hook. By sheer chance both my girlfriend and I had failed to hang up properly, resulting in a staggering 11-hour call between Newcastle and India. I haven't seen the bill yet.

Disco shame

Fighting on the dance floor

It started out as the usual Friday night: beers, chatting and eventually a club. The week in question me and a few mates went to a club which had just opened. We were fairly drunk but by no means bladdered, but we did decide to have a game of 'spoof' – a variation on the paper/rock/scissors game – with the loser having to do the forfeit of his mates' choice. After I lost a round I was instructed to go onto the half-filled dancefloor and dance like, for want of a better word, a spaz. I duly went down in front of the speakers and jerked around, dragging my leg behind me in terrible taste. After several minutes I felt a vicious punch to my cheek, and turned around to fight the bastard who'd hit me. We exchanged hard blows for a solid minute, then the bouncers came over and dragged me out. A minute or so later my friends came out to find me black and blue, sitting dejectedly on the kerb, our fun evening over. It was then that my mates pointed out the lad I'd fought sported an orthopaedic shoe.

'Phone sex' faux pas

Caller compromises a friend

One night, having consumed too much alcohol and a greasy kebab, my mates and I retired to a friend's house to watch an 'adult' video. Struggling out of bed the next day, I decided to give one of the crew a ring. When he answered the phone, I began to repeat some of the dialogue from the film. 'Oooh, come on. Johnny, fuck me ... I want that big cock inside me ... that's it! Harder ... HARDER! You're so big!' The next thing I heard was the sound of a phone being slammed down; but, mysteriously, I could still hear my friend on the line, blathering away in a blind panic. His mother, a woman so strait-laced that she'd make Mother Teresa took like Tabatha Cash, had picked up the phone at the same time downstairs. So Mrs M, if you come across this piece, it was me who made the obscene phone call, and I'm sorry if you've spent years in torment about the sexual activities of your favourite son.

Cool driving blunder

Jilted man in getaway farce

My first serious girlfriend dumped me on Christmas Day. I'd driven to the house she shared with her mother to deliver her presents, and she broke the news in a typically blunt way. Distressed beyond words, I ran out to my car and decided I'd depart in a dramatic and memorable fashion. I jumped into my beaten-up Escort and attempted a fast-moving reverse flick out of her narrow driveway. Unfortunately, instead of flying backwards in a cloud of burning rubber, I deposited my car into her mother's prize flower bed.

This was bad enough, but, in my frantic attempt to escape before anyone noticed, the spinning back wheels dug themselves deeper into the soil. My now ex-girlfriend's mother attempted to push the car out. She then remembered she was asthmatic and quietly collapsed on the driveway. To make matters worse, I had to borrow £75 from her to pay for a tow truck – I'd spent all my money on the Christmas presents.

It transpired my 'ex' was meeting her new boyfriend that night, and was unable to get her car past the wreckage of mine, which was blocking the driveway.

Tea with milk?

Student recycles waste

While in my first year at university, I suddenly found myself extremely hard up, and so were my student housemates. As anyone who has shared a house will know, a certain amount of 'borrowing' of one another's food goes on. Normally I took this stoically, but as I was trying to live on £1.38 per week, I found I could bear it no longer. I had put up with it for several weeks, but the final straw came when someone in my house all but finished my carton of milk. Returning home drunk and looking forward to my evening meal (and lunch and breakfast) of Frosties, I found the milk was almost all gone. I hit the roof. Determined to teach the culprit a lesson, I pissed in the carton and went to sleep, still seething. I was awoken at midday by one of my housemates saying my parents had just arrived to visit. 'I made them a cup of tea, I used your milk,' she said. I had trouble facing my parents after that, especially since my father crashed the car while being violently sick on the drive home.

Names entered

Church remembers alive folk

On Remembrance Sunday last February, my friends and I decided to attend a small memorial service at a nearby village church. When we arrived, we filled in the visitors' book sitting in the foyer, purely because judging by the neatly printed surnames, everyone else in our small community had already entered their names. The service went very well until the padre began to read out the village dead, and we recognized the book he was reading from. Before he could get to our neatly printed names however, my friend cracked, turned to me and blurted out, 'We are going to hell for this, mark my words!' before bolting for the door. I just followed, shrugging my shoulders and tutting at

the padre. We later found out that our names were
indeed read out, and not one person noticed.

Selfish gym-goer

Sauna causes sap to rise

Last April, after completing a strenuous work-out at my local gym, I decided to spend a relaxing half-hour in the sauna. It had a lockable door with a large tinted glass window, the other side of which was the men's showers. Feeling selfish, I put the lock on and lay down to enjoy a bit of solitary sweating. An old chubby man then wandered into the showers and, after trying the sauna door, stood under a jet of water. I left him to it and closed my eyes until it was time to leave. When I opened my eyes however, I couldn't help but notice the old boy having the best wank of his life.

Worse, he was marvelling at his reflection in the door window. Then he suddenly waddled straight over and, with only a thin sheet of glass between my head and his angry Jap's eye, unleashed a thick torrent of gentleman's gel all over the window. I waited a good hour before I dared come out.

Blasphemous brother

Unsuspecting caller insulted

Last year I visited my sister for the weekend. We were chatting on Sunday afternoon when she told me that the Jehovah's Witnesses had been coming round week after week, and just didn't seem to take no for an answer. As we drank our coffee there was a knock at the door, and I told my sister I would deal with it. Sure enough, there on the doorstep was a clean-cut young chap with an armful of books. Before he could begin to bore me with his chatter I told him, quite loudly, to fuck right off, and slammed the door in his face. Seconds later there was another knock at the door, and I went back to answer it. 'Look, mate,' I said, 'I've told you once. Now do yourself a favour and fuck off.'

The young man remained very calm, although I noticed he turned rather red, and said: 'I'm the curate of St Cuthbert's Church, and am just checking to see that Vikki's (my niece) christening was satisfactory.'

Water fear

Natural obstacle spooks caver

The last caving expedition that I went on involved an unexpected 'sump' – a point where rock meets water. This particular obstacle was four foot long, and the only way past was to dive into the icy water and pull myself along a permanently fixed length of submerged rope. Easy enough, perhaps – except that I can't swim. Amazingly, however, I managed it, and enjoyed a full day's caving without incident. On the return leg, I again arrived at the ominous sump, and three of my mates dived under before tugging on the rope – the signal for me to go. I held my breath, screwed up my eyes and ducked underwater, frantically pulling my way to safety. As soon as I thought I was clear I raised my head, only to hit rock. I pulled myself further forward and tried again. More rock. Starting to panic, I made one last, desperate effort to save myself from drowning. To my amazement, I burst out of the water – only to be surprised to find that I was 20ft from the sump and completely alone.

My mates later told me that when I appeared from under the rock, they had stood either side of me and held a large boulder over my head, keeping pace with me as I dragged myself along the rope – before eventually adopting the 'scatter and divide' method to avoid a serious beating from a very scared caver.

Hole undammed

Elderly chubster enjoys motion

During the early Seventies I found myself in hospital with two broken legs. In the bed next to me lay a fat old man, who was in for chronic constipation. Every day after dinner, some poor nurse would have to stick a hose up his arse so that he could pass solids. Obviously this made him very irritable, so I used to rub salt in the wound with a cheerful announcement of, 'That was a great crap!' whenever I used the bedpan. The time came when I was finally allowed to leave, and I told the old boy that I would miss watching his daily hour of discomfort. He grumpily informed me that he needed a shit, but before I could summon a nurse, someone had a heart attack in the corner, and everyone scooted away to help. All alone, he pushed his generous arse out off the bed, until I was within kissing distance of it, and proceeded to empty his bowels onto the floor in front of me. A humungous pile of brown, black and red shit rose up off the tiles, and when he had finished he pulled his arse back in, turned to me with watering eyes and said, 'What a great crap that was!'

Kitchen horror

Secret ingredient destroys love supper

Last year I was lucky enough to meet a beautiful girl at a party. I was even luckier when the girl – a model I had thought to be well out of my league – actually seemed to enjoy my company. Fully seizing the one and only opportunity in my life to make it with a stunner, I spent every second of the evening with her, and was shocked when my invitation to come to supper the following week was accepted. She told me she was a vegetarian and I spent the week devising the perfect meal. But while I was cooking my winter vegetable casserole I realized I didn't have any vegetable stock, so I bunged in a chicken stock cube, seasoned the whole thing heavily and prayed she wouldn't notice my deception. All went well. She ate a huge portion and complimented me on my cooking.

When I asked her how long she had been a vegetarian, she told me it had only been for a year and that she actually loved meat but had developed a severe allergy to animal fat, breaking out in hives every time she ate it. Sure enough, as the evening passed her face broke out in blotches and she began to get feverish. In the end I had to confess. Due to her state she missed a modelling assignment the next day, and has never spoken to me since.

Store drama

Biker bothers shopper

When I was younger I was into motorbikes in a big way, and after yet another strip-down of my 50cc, I headed down to my local dealer to order some parts. While I was standing in the queue, dreamily watching the young girl working behind the counter, one of the shop dummies, complete with helmet, boots, jacket and gloves, fell over. The young shop assistant quickly came over and picked it up, and we had a laugh about it while I ordered my parts. Returning the next day to collect them I took my place behind a mean-looking man, who was dressed as if he had just stepped off the set of *Mad Max*. Again I soon found myself staring at the shop assistant, completely lost in thought, when suddenly the biker in front of me moved. Unfortunately, I had a sudden flashback to the previous day – and before I knew what I was doing I reached forward and grabbed him tight round the stomach. We wrestled for quite a long time before I came to my senses; all I could muster as I looked into his furious eyes was:

'Sorry, I thought you were a dummy.'

Not surprisingly, I've never been back.

Tattoo screw-up

Man scarred forever

For several years I had wanted a tattoo, but never liked a design enough to make the commitment. Then, last year, a Japanese student attended the college I go to, and we became friends. I introduced him to the lads, and we all had a great year. When he had to leave, he gave each of us a beautifully designed card with the Japanese characters of our names printed on them. My name looked really cool in Japanese script, so I decided to tattoo it on my shoulder.

Everyone said how great it looked, and I was really pleased ... until I went to Sicily this April, when I took the opportunity to show off my tat on the beach. We were challenged to a game of volleyball by some

Japanese girls who kept screaming 'Sidney!' at me – which was odd, as it's my best friend's name. Yep, the cards had been switched, and I now have my mate's stupid name scrawled across my shoulder.

Filthy kiwi

Bloke leaves his mark on bed

After leaving university I moved into a flat with a group
of friends – one of whom I was pretty keen on. We had
been in the flat a couple of weeks and I felt I was
making good headway. One night a few of us,
including the girl I fancied, were sitting around in my
room chatting and having a few drinks. Trying to be
laid-back and cool I was wearing an ilavalava – a
Samoan version of the kilt, worn by both men and
women. After a while we ran out of drinks and I
volunteered to go to the local boozer to get more.
I figured nobody wanted a shot of my balls as I stood
up, so I slid delicately across the bed. On coming back
with the beers I saw that the two blokes in the room

had tears of mirth running down their faces, while the two girls were ashen-faced. I also noticed a book sitting in the middle of the bed. I picked it up and was shocked and embarrassed to find that, while sliding off the bed, rather than keeping my dignity I managed to lose it all by leaving a 4-inch shit stain on the duvet. I did, eventually, get it on with my flatmate, but it took four weeks of hard work to put the memory of the fudge strip firmly out of her mind.

Button pushed

Man brings events to a standstill

On what seemed like the hottest day of last summer, while on a particularly tedious and potentially relationship-destroying trip around the local shopping centre with my wife, I found myself stuck on a packed escalator, unable to move due to a large group of coffin-dodgers blocking the route ahead. The escalator seemed to be moving exceptionally slowly and, with sweat running off my head and into my eyes, I suddenly reached the end of my tether. Before I could stop myself, my hand reached out and punched the bright red emergency stop button – a move which brought the moving stairway to an immediate halt. People, including the frail old pensioners, crashed forwards into each other, sending bags and packages flying off in all directions. But amazingly, the crime was never pinned on me. The last thing I remember as I trod over the heap of bodies to escape the carnage was a desperate plea from an innocent little boy, who was being soundly thrashed for 'being so bad'.

Strange instructions

Patient stands proud

A few years ago, while working in America, I was struck down with kidney stones and rushed to a plush American hospital for a series of tests. My company was paying the bill, so no expense was spared, and I was appointed my own personal, and attractive, female attendant. I had to lie naked on a table, following instructions such as, 'Tackle to the left please, scrotum to the right,' while my nether-regions were photographed.

This was fine until she completely stunned me with the line, 'The doctor would like some of you erect.' She said that she would be back in a few minutes. I then set about raising steam but by the time she

came back, the best I had mustered was a lazy lob.
She then pointed to another machine standing in the
corner. 'I need you to stand up straight for an X-ray,'
she said, tears streaming down her face.

Flatmate required

Kindly offer rejected

Just over a year ago I had to find a new flatmate, and ended up scanning the university noticeboard. Among the scruffy notes from homeless students was one from a man named 'Jesus'. I proceeded to phone my list of prospective flatmates, but Jesus wasn't in, so I left a message on his answering machine asking him to come around that evening at nine. I then settled down in front of the TV to wait for the other interviewees to turn up, but nobody came – until, at nine, the doorbell rang. Assuming that Jesus had got the message and decided to come round, I buzzed the guy in and stood at the top of the communal stairwell to greet him. Unlike the kindly, bearded chap I had expected, he was a big, mean-looking man, and I nervously stuck out my hand. 'Hello,' I said. 'Are you Jesus?' He must have stared at me for a full minute before slowly replying, 'No, my name is Heinrich.'

Convinced that Jesus was on his way up the stairs and unable to lower my arm through sheer nerves, I looked over his shoulder and said quietly, 'Oh, I was expecting Jesus. Never mind, would you like to come in and see my room?' Without taking his eyes off me, the bloke edged down the stairs, one by one, and left.

As I found out next day, the girls living above me were also advertising their flat and Heinrich had been on his way up to view it.

Ballgirl taunted

Tennis ball fells player

Many years ago my mate Peter asked if I would like to come and play tennis with him at his local club. Neither of us had played much tennis before, so Pete just hit balls at me as hard as he could, which I tried in vain to smash back. Our amateur attempts didn't go unnoticed by the two women on the court next to us, who spent most of the game giggling. And then it happened. One of them started walking towards us to retrieve a ball, just as Pete hammered back a shot.

But instead of coming to me, it shot off to the left, straight into the head of the approaching woman, who went down like a sack of shit. There was a stunned silence as we all stared at her in disbelief, broken only by Peter, who was completely oblivious to what he had done, and without looking up, cheerfully shouted, 'Thanks, lady!' as his ball rolled gently to a halt at his feet.

Scorer mix-up

Player both on & off pitch

My first assignment as a budding football reporter on
my local rag was to cover a game between Sheffield
Wednesday and Blackburn. Things started badly before
I even got there, when I became mired in traffic about
a mile from the ground. I decided to abandon it, and
sprinted towards the floodlights. With seconds to spare
I barged into the press room, where my dishevelled
appearance caused a ripple of laughter from the
seasoned reporters and took a seat next to a man
from BBC Radio Lancashire and his guest summarizer.

Only then did I realize that I had forgotten my team-
sheet, but found it easy to guess what was going on,
until a sudden goal caused chaos in the press box as

everyone disagreed whose foot had put the ball in the back of the net. Sensing a chance to impress my new media colleagues, I cleared my throat and said confidently, 'It was Kevin Gallagher.' There was a murmur of thanks as the journos jotted the name down, and my proud face must have looked a picture when Radio Lancashire's guest summarizer leaned over, nudged me and said, 'I'm Kevin Gallagher.'

Furniture frolics

Man disturbs tea run

One night my girlfriend and I decided to christen my mum's new sofa, while she was out on the town with a few friends. After the session I dropped the now full Durex into the nearest thing available – a used tea mug – and we settled down in front of the television.

Mum came home with a couple of her friends, and they sat in the kitchen to have a cup of tea and a chat. Needing some more cups, mum popped into the lounge and rounded up the few on the table, including the one that contained our little 'present', while we sat oblivious on the couch, engrossed in what was on the box. One boiled kettle later, we heard screaming from the kitchen, and what sounded remarkably like someone being sick.